Dear Darl ♡
thanks
enjoy
Toni

VALIDATE ME QUICK, I'm Double Parked!

another *Shirley, You Can Do It!* book

by

Toni Sorenson Brown

Library of Congress Catalog Card Number:
95-71765
ISBN: 0-9644552-9-3

Published by TOKEN INK
P.O. Box 2246
Provo, Utah 84603 801-373-4718

For

Every woman who can relate to Shirley,
especially Janis, Georgia, Marda,
Evelyn and Eva.
You are my friends and inspiration.

*This book is most effective when shared aloud
woman to woman.
However, anyone can enjoy and engage in the episodic
evolution of Shirley.*

The shrill screech of the alarm shattered the dark morning silence. Shirley shot up in bed. "Who died?" she screamed into the buzzing telephone receiver.

Her husband grunted and jabbed her in the ribs with his elbow. "It's the alarm clock."

Reality slowly came in to focus.

5 a.m.

Monday morning.

The start of a new woman.

Shirley rocked the phone receiver back on to the hook and slapped the snooze button on the alarm.

"Shirley, you're not getting up *now*?" Stan muttered, more into his pillow than at her.

Shirley sighed, "Uh, uh."

It was still pitch black outside when she managed to drag herself from the bedroom to the bathroom. She flipped on the light switch. BIG mistake. It felt like someone had just yanked her eyeballs from their sockets, pulled them out far enough to challenge their elasticity and then let 'em flap back into place.

"So this is what early morning euphoria is like," she mumbled, splashing cold water on to her sleep-swollen face.

2

By 6 a.m. the sun still wasn't up, but Shirley was wide awake. She had already made it through the first three goals on her "things to do today" list. She was feeling pretty good about herself, a foreign feeling for this woman.

No, this wasn't the *first* attempt at becoming a new woman. But it was the first day of *this* effort, and this time would be different she felt her womanly seventh sense reassure her. "*Surely*, you can do this," she whispered aloud, then chuckled, "*Shirley*, you can do this!"

When 7 a.m. rolled around the rest of the family was just stumbling from slumber. She couldn't help feeling a twinge of nervous anticipation. What would they think when they saw all that she had accomplished? There was her exercised and showered body (a major work still in progress) the makeup (lips actually lined before dark), the vacuumed carpet (with no ground in

3

Cheerios or even footprints showing), and the crowning master piece: the sparkling kitchen. The table was set with real linen napkins and Sunday dishes. There was fresh squeezed orange juice in frosted mugs. Healthy home baked oat bran muffins and steaming cracked wheat cereal sweetened with honey were Shirley's main attractions.

Aesthetically pleasing *and* healthy, she thought proudly.

Shirley stood at the bottom of the staircase, anxiously awaiting the delight that was sure to register on her family's faces as they raced down the stairs.

"Where's my math paper?" shouted Sean, racing right past Shirley in a whirly blur.

"It's on the desk, dear," she answered, telling herself that he was *only* seven. He could be excused.

Next came Samantha. " The table looks nice. What's for breakfast?"

"Orange juice, muffins and cereal," Shirley announced proudly.

"Healthy stuff, huh?" Samantha managed that whiney sarcasm that only a twelve-year-old can. "Got any toast - *white* bread?"

5

Breakfast was even *more* than Shirley could have dreamed.

Her husband Stan enjoyed his bacon, eggs and *white* toast.

"I'm just not in the mood for cracked wheat," he'd attempted an apology.

Then he kissed her on the cheek. It was one of those puckered, dry "duty" kisses. There was no devotion in his lips, or in his compliment.

"Shirley, you've outdone yourself this morning," said Stan, squeezing catsup over his eggs.

"My feelings exactly," she agreed.

Samantha enjoyed her toast and did sample the orange juice. "This tastes different," she said, whining again. "And it's got feathers floating in it."

"That's because it's fresh squeezed," Shirley explained calmly, digging her freshly painted fingernails into palms.

"I like the frozen kind in a can," Samantha said, gulping it anyway. "It tastes better ."

"I'll remember that next time," Shirley said, vowing that she *certainly* would.

Sean, bless his seven-year-old heart, ate three of Shirley's oat bran muffins smothered in fresh strawberry jam. He too, wasn't in the mood for cracked wheat.

But he did think the frosted goblets were a "cool" effect, especially when Shirley didn't lunge quite fast enough to keep Sean from pouring microwaved steaming hot cocoa into his.

"I'll help you clean it up," Shirley's husband Stan said of the shattered glass mess.

"That's okay, I can do it."

"I'll help you, Mommy," volunteered Sara, who was three years old, and at the moment, aeons more mature than Shirley.

"No honey, you could cut yourself," she cautioned just before blood spurted from Shirley's index finger.

B y the time 10 a.m. rolled around, Stan was off to work, Samantha and Sean were at school and Sara was coloring creatures she had made out of the cracked wheat box. Turns out *nobody* was really in the mood for such a hearty cereal. Not even Shirley. But she did manage to finish off the muffins and an entire bottle of apricot preserves. Then Shirley sat at her Macintosh to tackle her latest freelance job.

Suddenly she felt like it was midnight and her body slumped in her chair. Why did her life have to be experienced in such extremes, she wondered. This morning's high and this minute's low. It seemed she was always tipping one end of the scale or the other. Why couldn't she manage to just enjoy the measures in between?

Shirley sat staring at the blank computer screen, feeling a little profound, but mostly down. Then she heard the voice. It was a man's voice. She shook her head to clear her thoughts, then listened. Sara had turned the TV on and the noise was blaring from down the hallway.

"For any woman who longs to feel worthwhile, appreciated ,and complete. Stay tuned."

Shirley was there in a heartbeat.

Sounds like one I can't miss, she told herself, adjusting the volume and falling back into the comfort of the couch cushions.

For the next sixty minutes Shirley sat mesmerized while Sara continued to color. She was so engrossed in the program that Shirley didn't even notice when Sara traded her crayons in for the lip liner that had been so enormously *in*effective that morning.

The infomercial man was captivating. This male Ph.D. on women's emotions carefully explained what was missing from Shirley's life: VALIDATION.

How could a stranger know her so well? He was absolutely right. No one made Shirley feel worthwhile, appreciated, or complete. She lacked that stamp of approval that somehow made her a legitimate success.

She wasn't a broken woman, but she certainly was bruised.

Validate Me Quick!

When the 1 900- VAL-DATE number flashed across the screen, Shirley recognized it for what it was. But she was desperate and $3.95 per minute sounded like a pretty good investment at the moment.

She felt a little foolish dialing the number and almost hung up when she heard a recorded message announce, "Stay on the line for information that is sure to change your life."

Shirley wanted her life changed so she stayed on the line. She felt like she had been hanging for so long now anyway, what was another minute or two.

Seven dollars and ninety cents later she spoke to an actual person. Twenty-two minutes, or a week's worth of groceries later, Shirley had the basic formula for validation. It was simple really. Almost silly. But if it would make her feel better about herself, what did she have to lose?

The formula seemed elementary enough. All Shirley had to do was to acquire a real parking validation coupon, or make one of her own. Then she had to divide it into pieces like a jigsaw puzzle. On each piece she was supposed to write down the name of a person from whom she sought validation. When she finally felt validated by them she was to put the puzzle together piece by piece until it was complete- and abracadabra, so was Shirley.

"I can do this," she assured herself aloud. "Can Mommy borrow a page from your coloring book?" Shirley asked Sara.

"What are you doing, Mommy?" asked Sara, her lips, eyes and eight of her fingernails covered with Shirley's Magical Mauve lip liner.

"I'm going to feel validated."

Sara's little brow furrowed. "Will it hurt?"

Shirley smiled, licked her thumb and began to smear the lip liner across her daughter's face. "I sure hope not, Honey. I sure hope not."

*S*hirley was sure the list would be a short one. First there was Stan. She loved him desperately, but he never even came close to understanding , let alone appreciating all that she did in any given day. No, he did not comprehend the fact that she had put her career on hold to help raise their family. She ran the house. Nurtured the kids. Supplemented their income. Cooked. Cleaned. Chauffeured.

Naw, Stan did not validate her.

But he would.

Next came the kids. If only they could grasp the fact that all her loony behavior like screaming and scolding was not because she was insane, but because she loved them. Putting it into words suddenly sounded a little crazy, but Shirley told herself she did deserve their respect. She was their mother. They needed to recognize her role in their lives. Not slave, but mother.

Still, how do you seek validation from a three-year-old, she questioned.

Good thing Shirley still had that 1-900 number.

It was three days later before Shirley had completed her validation puzzle list. The length of the list surprised her, but a few of the names that turned up on it actually stunned her. Some had been written, then erased, rewritten, scratched out, and then inked in again.

Besides Stan and the kids, there was Shirley's mother. Theirs was a relationship that would have perplexed Freud. But any mother/daughter relationship was complicated, Shirley reassured herself. Daughters needed to be validated by their mothers, so Shirley felt good about giving her mother a significant piece of the puzzle.

Shirley's old boss was one of those names she wrote with a hesitant hand. Even after all the time that had passed since he had fired her, the man could still make her tremble and sick to her stomach.

"Maybe I need more than a do-it-yourself course," Shirley mused aloud to little Sara as they sat at the kitchen table, carefully crafting the validation puzzle. Each piece was meticulously written and designed. Sara's crayons, colored pencils and bright markers provided individuality to each piece. All of the names were written in black ink, but some were definitely larger and bolder than others.

The name of Shirley's former boss looked like it had been written with a huge black crayon, but only because it had been.

"How come that piece of your puzzle is darker than the others?" Sara wanted to know.

Dark was a good word to describe that piece and all that it represented.

"Can Mommy borrow your fattest black marker?"

Shirley outlined that one name over and over and over again until only she could read it.

Another name that Shirley wrote with trepidation was also from her past. It was Shirley's tenth grade English teacher. The woman had been Shirley's mentor, although Shirley was painfully aware that the teacher never considered her a prized pupil.

She still had the report on Chaucer, the one with the teacher's bloody red cursive across the top stating: "There is no shame in being *average*. Grade: **C**."

That one message had left an indelible impression on Shirley's young mind - on her life, and it was *way* past time to set the record straight.

There were other names that belonged. Names that were natural pieces of the puzzle - friends and family. Wanting to feel validated by them made sense.

But why, wondered Shirley, were there pieces of her most personal puzzle, devoted to her hair stylist and the family milkman?

Why did she care what near-strangers thought of her?

Why did it matter?

She had no answers. She only knew it mattered very much to her.

When Shirley had completed the puzzle she carefully cut out each piece with Sara's blunt scissors.

Every step of the project so far had been cathartic. But then there had been no real contact with any of the names on the puzzle. No confrontations.

Shirley hated confrontation.

Maybe this is all I need, she thought, feeling a little like she was on the third day of antibiotics. Better, but not well.

Okay, I'll do it. I'll go to each one of these people and seek validation.

But what if they won't. . .

She quickly caught her negativism and squelched it. Then she placed each puzzle piece in an envelope and tucked it in her lingerie drawer - under the red and black teddies that she still kept, though she hadn't worn them in a decade.

Validate Me Quick!

Two weeks later that envelope was still in the bottom of the drawer.

There had been no more 5 a.m. wake up calls, but the metamorphism of Shirley was still under way.

Cold cereal and white toast - actually anything that could pop from the toaster - sufficed for breakfast. No one seemed to miss the "feathers" in the orange juice or the cracked wheat cereal.

The minimum weekly exercise requirements Shirley had set for herself were sometimes met and sometimes let go.

She found if she attempted to chart her progress on a daily basis, it was too disheartening. But if she allowed herself some time and space, Shirley could see that she was headed in the right direction.

Maybe this validation thing isn't necessary after all, she about had herself convinced.

Then the doorbell rang.

"Mom! I was just thinking about you - sort of."

Shirley's mother half-hugged her daughter, "That's nice - I suppose." Then she quickly pushed past Shirley."I was in town for a doctor's appointment. I thought I'd stop by and see the kids. Where are they?"

She looked around the kitchen and focused on the table. It was still covered with breakfast dishes although it was practically lunch time.

Shirley tried to ignore the sneer she was sure registered on her mother's face. "You know that the kids are at school. Now what about a doctor's appointment?" she asked. "What's wrong?"

"Don't worry, Dear," Shirley's mother answered, gingerly picking up a half eaten pop-tart and dropping it onto a plate, then stepping back as if were a grenade. "So where's little Sara?"

Shirley couldn't help it. She followed her mother's lead like well trained pet. She started cleaning the kitchen table, piling all of the partially eaten breakfast treats onto a plate and then into the garbage. "Sara is at a neighbor's playing. Now tell me about your doctor's appointment."

"Do you have a *clean* dish cloth?" her mother avoided the question with a question.

Shirley felt the muscles in her neck tighten. This tug-o-war was an all-too familiar game they played. Shirley always lost.

But not this time. She handed her mother a fresh rag from the bottom drawer. "Have at it, Mom."

Eleven minutes and thirty nine seconds, and one feud under the belt later, Shirley discovered that her mother had just had her annual mammogram.

"I told you it was nothing to worry about," she said a little defensive.

"Sit down, Mom," said Shirley, deciding there would never be a perfect time. But now was as good as any other. "I've got something I want to talk to you about."

When Shirley came back from the bedroom she was carrying an envelope.

"What is it, some kind of new diet?" Shirley's mother asked.

Shirley bit her lip until she was sure she could taste blood. "No, Mom. But it is going to help me get rid of some extra baggage." With that snappy comment Shirley suddenly realized she was on her own. Those $3.95 minutes had been a rip-off. No one had told Shirley HOW to *seek* validation.

"Well, what is it then?" her mother sounded impatient.

"It's my validation puzzle."

"Your *what*?"

"It's my attempt to feel validated by the people in my life who take me for granted. You know, I just want to feel acknowledged and appreciated."

"Don't we all?" her mother mumbled, but Shirley wasn't listening to anything but the pounding of her heart.

Shirley sat next to her mother at the now sparkling kitchen table and simply blurted out her deepest harbored feelings. What she had wanted to say to her mother ever since she was a child. "I hate buttermilk!"she shouted.

Shirley's mother simply stared at her daughter for the longest minute of Shirley's life. Then in that what's-wrong-with-you tone, she said, "Shirley, you're just having a bad day."

900 number or not, she met her mother's gaze. "No, Mom. I'm actually having a pretty good day. There are just a few things I want you to know. Most of all - I love you. I really do. And I am very much like you, but I am not you. I don't wash the dishes before I put them in the dishwasher. What's the point? I buy my Thanksgiving rolls frozen in a plastic bag. I'm afraid of the sewing machine." Shirley took a deep breath. This was not easy.

"And I am very well aware of the fact that I am overweight. So there is no need for you to remind me every time we are together."

Another long and awkward pause seemed like it would never end. Then Shirley's mother asked quietly, "Is that it?"

Shirley sighed, "Yes, that's it."

"Okay, now I have something for you. I love you, too. Really I do. More than you can ever know. Sometimes I say the wrong things. Sometimes I do things that hurt you. I'm truly sorry for those times. It's just that we are so different. . . "

"Exactly! agreed Shirley. "That's the point! You are walking tradition. I am the tradition breaker."

"That's one of the things I like about you," confessed Shirley's mother.

The next silence was the longest one. But no words were needed as mother and daughter embraced in the most spontaneous hug they had ever experienced.

32

Shirley was positive she had finally broken through. Her mother loved her and accepted her for what she was. This validation stuff really was a breeze.

Shirley's mother was the first to back away from the hug."May I ask you something while we are being so open with each other?"

"Sure, Mom." Shirley hadn't felt this close to her mother since she was ten. "Ask me anything."

But even as she invited the query, she also braced herself . Conditioned response or instinct. Either way Shirley's defenses went up.

"What's with all the "S" names in your family? Shirley's mother asked.

This time it was Shirley's turn to stare at her mother. "What's that suppose to mean?" she finally asked, the week's growth of hair on her legs and under her arms, bristling.

33

"Nothing. Nothing at all," her mother backed down. "I've just wondered about the novelty of it and I've never dared ask before."

"So are you saying you don't like our kids' names?"

"No, that's not what I'm saying at all. I have just wondered if your name was Zenith and Stan's was Zeus, would your kids all have "Z" names?"

"Maybe. Would that affect how you felt about them?"

"Shirley, you're being silly now. I was just curious, that's all. I'm sorry I offended you. But have you ever stopped to think that *your* mother might need validation, too? I like to be included. Consulted, even. It's no fun making a child your whole life only to have that child grow up and exclude you from her adulthood."

34

"I'm sorry, Mom. I never knew you felt that way." Shirley apologized.

They spent the next thirty minutes learning things about each other that neither had suspected. Then Sara came home and Grandma went out to watch her roller blade. Shirley finished the document that was due the next day. Then she dumped a can of soup over some skinless chicken breasts and popped them in the oven.

"Do you want to stay and have supper with us?" Shirley invited her mother.

"No, I don't think so. For some reason I feel like that wrung out dirty dish rag of yours. I think I'll go home and have a shower and go to bed."

"Sounds like a great idea to me," said Shirley, feeling very much the same.

Shirley was a little unsure of what to do with that first piece of the puzzle. Had her mother actually validated her? She *had* acknowledged the fact that Shirley's feelings were justified; they'd even discussed the values of their diversity. But still, Shirley was a little unsure. It seemed there should be more. There was more. Maybe there was *always* more.

Validation does work both ways,Shirley was thinking when the telephone rang early the next morning. It was her mother.

"I've been thinking about something you said. Shirley, We're not all that different."

"You're right," admitted Shirley.

Her mother sounded pleased "We agree on more than you realize. "Besides, I have a confession. I hate buttermilk, too."

Shirley was shocked. "Then why on earth do you guzzle it by the gallon? And why did you make *me*?"

"Because when I was a girl, my mother drank it and she told me the same story I passed on to you. But listen to this. I called *my* mother this morning and asked her "why all the buttermilk?" Know what she said?"

"What?"

"In her day and age they didn't have electric refrigerators and they milked their own family cows each day. They had to hurry and drink the buttermilk they made before it spoiled. Turns out she hates the nasty stuff, too. It's just that her mother made her drink it and so she made me and I made you and don't you dare make Samantha or Sara.

"I couldn't even if I tried," laughed Shirley, feeling that that first piece of her puzzle fit perfectly.

A few nights later Shirley called the kids into her room.

"Are we in trouble?" they wanted to know.

"No, but I think *I* am."

It had been just another day in the life of Shirley. Up and at it before the rest of the family. Breakfast, two sack lunches, three batches of laundry, two loads to the dishwasher (Okay, so it was the same load twice - she forgot the soap the first time). A hunt for a missing school report, two trips to school and back, one to the bank, one to the dry cleaners. Soccer practice. A piano lesson. A preschool parent-teacher conference.

Somewhere in the middle of all the "go-get-'em" was also a lot of guilt. She had started with the best of intentions. One half bagel - no cream cheese. Two of her eight required glasses of water. There had been a glimmer of hope some time that morning. And there was the promise she made to herself to exercise "just as soon as I have a break."

A mad dash around the neighborhood did manage to accelerate her heart rate. The family dog was in heat and the little tramp had decided to go socializing.

Shirley finally found her down the block in a garage with a Doberman. Shirley somehow managed to pry them apart and to drag their dachshund home. She immediately locked her in the bathroom.

The entire episode left Shirley famished and all she could find was a leftover chocolate glazed donut.

Of course she felt guilty, but she had to think about that later. She was facing three deadlines for her desktop publishing company.

Guilt could wait. Guilt could *always* wait.

Stan called and asked her to pick up a part for the family boat that hadn't been on the water in years. Oh, and if she wasn't doing anything else, could she gas up the car and run it through the wash?

When Shirley picked Sara up from preschool the poor child was starving, so out of concern and compassion, Shirley took her to McDonald's for a Happy Meal.

Shirley could not be rude to the man at the drive up who asked, "Would you care to try one of our combo meals today?"

After a Big Mac attack came another wave of guilt. This one too, had to be brushed aside.

Validate Me Quick!

There was shopping to do, dinner to prepare, envelopes that needed to be stuffed for the P.T.A. The phone rang 13 times. 4 were wrong numbers. Three were generated by computerized salesmen. Twice Shirley's mother called.

"Shirley, we're finally bonding!"

There were more dirty dishes. A broken plate. Sara wanted to make a horse stable out of popsicle sticks and so she took everything out of the freezer to thaw. Sean needed a new pair of soccer shoes - by practice time tomorrow. Samantha was in a fight with her best friend - so she needed her mother's consolation.

Stan did call - to say he was working late and wouldn't be home for dinner.

The doorbell rang for the seventeenth time. It was the little neighbor boy. "Can Sara play?" he asked for the seventeenth time that day.

Shirley loved her family. Her husband and children meant everything to her. It's just that she felt overwhelmed and under-appreciated. They expected *so* much from her. There were times she thought of getting in the car and driving away. She could never abandon them, but this mothering business was a full-time position. There were no breaks. She was always on call.

It was about time they started validating her feelings, her needs, and her contributions to their lives. If they weren't sure just exactly what those contributions were, Shirley was prepared to clarify.

Now she sat on the bed next to her kids.

"What' s wrong, Mom?" Samantha wanted to know..

Shirley wasn't sure where to begin. "Do you know how much I love you?"

"Yeah," they all responded.

"How do you show people that you love them?" she asked.

Sara raised her hand and shouted at the same time, "You hug them!"

"Good, Honey."

"You do stuff for them," answered Sean.

Shirley smiled wearily. "What do *I* do for you kids that shows how much I love you?"

Samantha didn't hesitate. "You listen to us."

"You come to watch my soccer games," said Sean, "even when the coach doesn't put me in."

"You read to me, and do those funny voices,"added Sara.

This wasn't at all what Shirley had expected. "What about big home cooked meals?" she asked. "And the clean house?"

Samantha and Sean looked at each other with uncertainty.

"You're a yummy cook, Mommy.!" said Sara.

"We love your dinners and the house always looks nice," Samantha agreed, "but sometimes after you cook and clean you are too tired and ..."

". . . grumpy!" Sean finished the thought. "That's why we love hot dog nights. You always have time to play Monopoly and baseball with us after."

It was a good thing it was Friday night because everyone stayed up way past their bedtime. Talking. Talking about the things that mattered most.

Not the kitchen floor that was so clean you could eat off it.

Not the sparkling toilet bowls.

Not the fancy souffles that took all day to prepare.

No, they talked about the little adventures the family went on together. The day Shirley made a home made slide out of a piece of painter's plastic and the garden hose. They didn't mention the expensive fancy holiday outfits that Shirley had worked and scrimped and saved for. They remembered the tie dyed T-shirts they made together in the sink one afternoon .

Shirley learned more about herself and her children that night than she could have in a lifetime of professional parenting courses.

Her kids weren't the ones who imposed so many demands on her. Shirley did that to herself. Of course they did require a great deal of her time and energy, but they cherished *her* more than what she did for them.

They didn't need anything fancy or elaborate. They needed *her*. And in spite of her doubts, they did appreciate her.

Shirley suddenly felt overwhelmed with peace and contentment. Three more pieces of her puzzle were complete. At least for tonight anyway.

"I love you because you took me to McDonald's and then we had a picnic on the lawn," Sara said, breaking the peace of that moment.

Reality returned.

"You took her to McDonald's and not us!" the other two children screamed their protest.

When Stan came home he found his wife and children all cuddled on their bed sleeping soundly. It looked like they had been having a party - catered by McDonald's.

*S*hirley was carefully gluing each piece of the validation puzzle on to a sturdy piece of matte board. The puzzle was coming together, slowly, but steadily. She intended to have it professionally framed when the last piece was complete.

In the meantime, Shirley's former boss was too much on her mind. Why had she ever included him in her life again? That chapter was over. Or at least it would be by the end of the afternoon.

Shirley had landed her first real job during her senior year of college. As the aid to the dean of psychology. What a break! Shirley was considering a career in counseling, and she viewed this as a tremendous opportunity to learn from a brilliant man whom everyone so respected and admired.

During that first month Shirley fed lab rats and cleaned cages. She graded tests and filed papers. She organized the office. She answered phones and arranged the professor's schedule. She even came in early so she could have steaming black coffee ready when he arrived.

This was her golden opportunity and she intended to make the most of it.

At the end of that first month, the man who could lecture for hours on the human condition, had never once called Shirley by name. He had not thanked her or even acknowledged her presence, except to leave notes chiding her when she didn't meet his expectations.

So he's reserved, she told herself.

So he's distant, she excused him six months later. At least now he was criticizing her face to face.

A year into the job Shirley excused his deteriorating conduct by attributing it to his intellect - and her lack of intelligence.

He was superior.

She was inferior.

She even made excuses for him when she felt he touched her inappropriately. He didn't mean anything by it.

When he ripped the cover page from a grant proposal she had written, then replaced it with his own name and credentials, Shirley kept silent. After all, she told herself, she did work for him. Maybe he had the right to do it.

But when the school got the grant money and he took all the credit, she did muster the courage to say, "I think you should have at least mentioned me in your speech."

It was the first time he ever called her by name. "Shirley, you're mistaken."

Why she stayed on for another twelve months only supported his observation. She *was* dumb.

When he fired her he did it by moving his office across campus - without telling her. Shirley showed up for work one Monday morning and the janitor informed her. "That guy's been promoted to administration These past couple of years he's really shined. He's worked hard for his new post. Do you know he landed a million dollar government grant?"

Shirley managed a nod. She didn't trust her voice because her throat suddenly felt like she had swallowed a brillo pad.

Then she tracked him across campus, and had the privilege of a one-on-one, only because he was coming down the narrow hallway, and there was no place to run.

"Professor, I don't understand," she said, cursing that quiver in her voice.

He did not look at her. "That's not surprising. My career is now headed in a different direction and there will not be a place for you. See the personnel office for your final check."

With that he walked past her, smashing her self-image with every fading step.

This was the most intelligent man Shirley had ever known. This was the man whose respect she had spent two years trying desperately to earn. Two years!

This was the man who had not treated her as "ordinary," but as a complete inferior.

Now Shirley sat in his plush executive office waiting for her scheduled 10 minute appointment.

It had been 15 years since Shirley had been left standing in that hallway without a job, and without any self-esteem.

"Am I supposed to know you?" he asked when he walked in the room.

He was old now and very tired looking. But his manner had not changed. Those old feelings of inferiority overwhelmed Shirley, but only momentarily.

Shirley reached out her hand as she introduced herself. He sat down at his desk without extending his own hand to her.

"What do you want?" he asked.

"Well Sir, I would like to tell you how I feel about the way I was treated while I was your assistant."

"Was there a problem?" He sounded a little less confident than Shirley ever remembered.

"As a matter of fact . . ."

Shirley knew time was short so she didn't waste a minute. She got right to the core. She poured out her heart, telling him how much her job had meant to her and how hard she had worked for him.

"I did a good job for you, Professor. Better than good. I wrote that grant and you took all the credit. There were other times when your behavior towards me was inappropriate. I didn't say anything then, but I am now."

He looked up from his desk. "There's a statute of limitations on such matters."

It took Shirley a full minute to realize what had just happened.

Validate Me Quick!

Shirley stood to leave, but first looked at him directly. She waited until his eyes finally met hers.

"You just don't get it, do you? You might be intelligent, but you're not very smart. Intellect will never replace integrity. Good-bye, Professor."

This time *he* was the one left alone.

Shirley glanced back one more time, just for a reality check, because the whole experience seemed sort of surreal, from his shriveled appearance, to her commanding voice, let alone the things that came out of her mouth! Who was this powerhouse in her body?

But there sat the professor. The intellectual giant himself. Was it Shirley's imagination or was the man actually shrinking. . .

59

When Shirley got out to her car she ripped that "dark" piece of her validation puzzle into confetti.

Why that man ever had any power over the way she felt about herself, Shirley could not imagine now. Her mistake.

It was also a mistake to think she needed his validation. He just wasn't worth it.

She now realized that she was the one who had given him power, and taking it back was all the validation she needed.

*I*t had been an eternity since Shirley's high school days. Mrs. Montgomery was about retirement age then, so Shirley wasn't exactly sure how she was going to track her down now.

One long distance phone call to Franklin High and she discovered a search wouldn't be necessary.

"I'm sorry, but Mrs. Montgomery passed away several years ago," Shirley was informed.

Late that night when the only sound in the house was the dryer down the hallway turning and turning, Shirley was lying in bed awake, thinking of Mrs. Montgomery.

A load of levis was set for the "less dry" cycle, and with each turn, the copper rivets hit against the metal barrel of the dryer. Actually, Shirley liked the rhythmic sound. It was soothing.

This was one of her most peaceful moments. With Stan snoring every once in awhile next to her and the kids all slumbering soundly, safe and home.

Shirley reached up and turned on the lamp next to her. Stan grunted his complaint at the light shining in his eyes.

"Turn over and go back to sleep," she said, scratching his back. "I'm going to be awake for awhile."

In the nightstand next to her bed was a large manila envelope. She unclasped it and dumped the contents out on her lap. There was the matte board with several of the validation puzzle pieces glued in place. There was another envelope containing the rest of the pieces.

Shirley sorted out Mrs. Montgomery's piece and then picked up the English report she had kept for all of these years.

She recalled how hard she had worked on that report. She had tackled Chaucer and had done it to please and impress Mrs. Montgomery.

Shirley had accomplished neither.

It wasn't the C grade that had whittled away at Shirley for all of these years. It was the judgement, written in Mrs. Montgomery's own hand.

"There is no shame in being average."

Average. Ordinary. Plain. Stupid.

Shirley was not just a C student; she was a C human being.

Up until that moment Shirley had lived her young life feeling rather special. Different. Unique. Filled with potential.

One comment changed her entire perception of herself.

After that it didn't matter how many other teachers gave her A's and B's and said, "Shirley, you have tremendous potential."

No, Shirley was just *average*.

And Mrs. Montgomery had been wrong.

There was great shame in being average.

Now for the first time since Shirley had read that remark, she could see the impact it had had on her adult life.

Because she had believed she was nothing special, she had treated herself as nothing special.

It was evident during those two years of torture, working for the professor. It was clear in her relationship with her family, particularly her mother. No matter what her mother meant, Shirley always interpreted her comments as some way of saying, "You are a disappointment to me."

Still, in spite of all that was average in her life, Shirley could not smother those moments of glory that were anything but ordinary.

Like the night Stan proposed, or those three magical moments when her body had produced two daughters and a son. She had been in full partnership with the Miracle Maker.

There were times when Shirley wondered what would fill her life if not for her husband and children. The thought made her uncomfortable, but tonight she realized she was much more than a mere extension of her family. She was the hub of the home, yes. But as an individual she was a bright, witty, warm and at times insightful woman.

Average? Hardly.

For one fleeting moment, she felt unworthy, but forced herself to pick up her pen instead of feeling sorry for herself.

Validate Me Quick!

Dear Mrs. Montgomery,
      You were the most influential teacher of my education, at least until now. I admired you, respected you, and hoped to emulate you.
      I don't know why I do that - latch on to certain people and allow them power to influence me. I certainly gave you carte blanche. When you labeled me as "average," I should have talked to you face to face. But after that, I don't believe I was ever able to make eye contact with you again.
      *But if you were standing in front of me tonight, Mrs. Montgomery, I would tell you that you were wrong. I am **not average**. In fact, I've never met an average person in my life. By God's own design, we are all unique individuals, with gifts to offer life and ways of giving that set us apart from one another. You taught school for thirty years. You should have known that.*

Validate Me Quick!

Today I feel extremely successful. I'm well into my second decade of marriage to a man whom I adore. I am the mother of three great kids, none of whom is average. I have friends. I have faith.

I own my own business. People pay me for my skills. I am ever learning. I am blessed.

In your eyes I may not amount to much, I may be just average, but I'm not looking through your eyes anymore.

"Turn off that light," Stan grumbled. "What are you doing anyway?"

"Writing a letter - to a dead woman."

Stan rolled on to his stomach and buried his face in the pillow. "Shirley, you're crazy," he yawned. "Surleee, you are."

Shirley folded the letter and put it in the manila envelope with all of her other validation paraphernalia.

Tomorrow she would glue another piece of the puzzle in place. But for now, the dryer had stopped, she had to get up and hang those Levis so they would finish drying straight and save her the task of ironing them.

Such an ordinary chore for such an extraordinary woman, she thought.

"I really am tired," she chuckled into the stillness of the night.

70

*T*he list was dwindling. Every few days another piece of the puzzle fit, or at least came close. Shirley was feeling the wholeness of the experience. Would it ever be truly complete? She didn't want her doubts to dance on her merriment. No way.

Even though the process seemed simplistic, perhaps juvenile, it was working. She could feel it.

She was getting to know herself better than she ever had. More importantly she liked herself better than she ever had.

71

The significant people on her puzzle list had been easier, in a way, than the casual acquaintances. It made sense that Shirley wanted and needed validation from her mother. It was perfectly reasonable that she wanted to set the record straight with her former boss. Her family and fiends were logical pieces to her validation puzzle. And she had always obsessed about her neighbors.

But her *hair stylist?* The *milkman?* The *girl* she hired to help with the house work? Why Shirley sought validation from them, she wasn't sure. But she did.

Shirley had a standing appointment with Debbie every six weeks. A cut and style was typical, but there was also the "highlight," "streaks," or "dye jobs" that her roots also required on a regular basis. A perm every now and then just to add some lift and volume was also part of the regime.

Debbie was young - 22 at the most. Single. Skinny - skinny. Adorable. She had perfect long, thick shiny hair. The kind Shirley would have killed for. Straight white teeth that any orthodontist would have been proud to say, "That smile is my work!"

And Debbie did smile a lot. In fact she laughed out loud at Shirley's jokes. No wonder Shirley liked her so much.

But there were things about Debbie that Shirley had to admit, drove her crazy. For one thing she wore heels eight hours a day and never complained.

For another, Debbie always wore Shirley's favorite color - basic black. On Shirley it seemed to scream that she was trying to hide something, or more like everything. But on Debbie it accentuated all the right parts. And Debbie had plenty of those. Her black jumpsuits, hot pants and miniskirts verified that. She kept a roll of masking tape at her styling station. She wrapped the tape around her hand, with the sticky side out, so she could keep her outfits hair-free and looking perfect.

Everything about Debbie seemed a little too perfect. Shirley wanted to hate her, but just couldn't because Debbie was so nice. Maybe that's why Shirley cared so much about what Debbie thought of her.

She was living Shirley's fantasy youth.

"Hi, Shirley," Debbie squeaked her usual enthusiastic greeting. "What are we doing today?"

Debbie was wearing black stretch pants, a white tee, and a black vest. No bra. *Everything* about Debbie was, well. . .perky.

Black pumps too. Her hair was done in some fancy French braid and her earrings matched her hair clip. Shirley felt very old and very dumpy in her baggy grey jogging suit and old Nikes.

"The usual," Shirley answered, but suddenly surprised herself with a change of mind. "No, I want something different. Something that doesn't remind me of my mother. Something. . ."

". . . Sassy?" Debbie suggested.

"Sounds good to me."

After their usual exchange of pleasantries - Shirley's kids and Debbie's ever-exciting love life - Shirley decided to launch right in.

"I really admire you, Debbie."

Debbie seemed surprised. "You admire me? Why?"

"Because you are always so happy. So pulled-together. So beautiful and talented. You spend eight hours a day helping people to feel better about themselves."

Debbie's expression showed she was deeply touched.

Shirley was just about to confess her own insecurities, about how she was positive Debbie must be disgusted with Shirley for letting herself go. Her no-style hair, her excess weight, her lack of makeup, her oversized and underrated wardrobe, her boring life. . . She was just about to justify it all - to the woman who did her hair. But Debbie broke Shirley's concentration.

"Shirley, you're the one *I* admire.

Now it was Shirley's turn to register surprise. "*Me*? Why?"

"Because you amaze me. You are a wife and a mother. You always talk about your family and your love for them is obvious. You have your own business. You are funny and smart. Every time you come in I learn something new from you. You're always reading and talking to people. You care about how you look, but you go so much deeper than just appearances. I always look forward to your appointments because I feel better about myself after you've been here."

There was no doubting Debbie's sincerity.

Once again Shirley had been wrong. There was no need to seek Debbie's validation - she already had it. She just hadn't realized it.

"What do you think of your new hair style?" Debbie asked Shirley, spinning the chair around to face the mirror.

Shirley studied her image carefully. She actually liked what she saw - the whole package.

"I love it," she said. "It looks *nothing* like my mother's."

After Debbie, the milkman was going to be easy. He always came between 7 and 7:30 a.m. Right when Shirley was yelling at the kids to "hurry and get ready or you'll be late for school." They were usually yelling back about not being able to find something they needed. It was chaos.

This morning the object of contention was a big pack of purple bubble gum and whether or not Sara could have it for breakfast. Shirley picked up a fit-pitching Sara and did her best to explain, "Grape gum does not count as one of your daily fruit requirements!"

80

On such mornings, Shirley was almost always still in her pj's with no makeup on and really scary morning hair.

She just *knew* the milkman thought she never fed her family anything except cold cereal for breakfast because half the time they had to wait for him to deliver before they could eat. And not always, but sometimes, he had to bill her twice to get paid. Shirley was sure the milkman thought she was a rotten wife, mother and person in general. For some reason, she worried about what he thought and was out to change his opinion.

Why she felt the need to justify herself and her life to him, she could not explain. But she did. It wasn't like they had any relationship at all. He was the milkman. She was the customer.

Still, "milkman" was one of the pieces of her puzzle. And she was out to complete the blasted thing now that she was *so* close.

So this morning she met him on the porch. She was wearing her skinny jeans - the ones she had to lay flat on her back to get zipped up. She had on a bright red blouse. Debbie had told her red was a power color. Her hair cut didn't look quite as good as it had when Debbie had done it, but it still looked good. So Stan hadn't noticed it. Big deal. Her lips and eyes were lined and she was wearing earrings and perfume.

"Good morning," she greeted the milkman cheerfully. "I know I was a little slow paying you last month, so here's this month's payment in advance."

He took the check and handed her two gallons of milk. "Thanks."

"Just in time for homemade French toast," she said. "My family loves my secret recipe. I put a teaspoon of vanilla in the batter."

He turned to leave.

"I know you must see me a mess every morning and hear me screaming," she said, following him to his truck. "I know you must think all I feed my family is Fruit Loops and Cheerios. I know you see me at my worst, you must see me as a real slob, but I'm not. Honestly, I'm not."

Shirley could have continued, but by now the motor was running and his hand was on the shifter.

He grinned down at her. "Actually, Ma'am I haven't given it a thought."

Shirley had to step back to keep from being hit as the milk truck continued down the street.

Stan met her halfway down the driveway.

"Shirley, *what* are you doing?"

"That's just what I was wondering," she confessed, laughing out loud at herself.

Stan looked at her, actually it was more of a stare. "Have you done something different with your hair?"

He noticed! Shirley grinned. "Yes I have. It's a little *sassy*, wouldn't you say?"

"Yeah, right. I especially like this effect," he said, tugging a huge wad of purple gum from her hair.

O kay, so she had been wrong about the milkman, too. It made Shirley promise herself she would never address another person by saying, "I know you must think. . ." So far that sure knowledge had batted her zero. She did NOT know what others thought, and to assume, she was realizing, was not her prerogative.

Once she realized that impressing the milkman was not crucial to her validation, Shirley thought about re-doing her puzzle. She was discovering that other people's opinions of her were a distant second to what she thought about herself.

Validate Me Quick!

On the afternoon that her weekly house cleaner was due, Shirley shut off her computer and got busy running her regular routine. She scrubbed toilets, vacuumed floors, dusted the mantel, and cleaned the glass in the China closet. She cleaned in preparation for the house cleaner. She always did. She couldn't stand the thought of anyone thinking she was a slob.

"I'm sorry this place is such a mess," Shirley apologized. "I've been so busy I've just had to let it go."

The young woman looked around at the freshly vacuumed carpets and the bleached kitchen countertops. "Don't worry about it."

Shirley struggled to keep her promise to herself. Instead of declaring, "I know you must think I'm lazy, filthy and a terrible homemaker," she did some fast rephrasing. "Do you think I'm lazy? Filthy? A terrible homemaker?"

The house cleaner looked at her like she was rabid.

Shirley hurriedly continued. "It's just that I feel so guilty for needing help. I feel inferior to all the women I know who work, raise families, and still maintain spotless homes."

"I haven't met any of those women in my line of work," she smiled at Shirley.

But Shirley was still on the needless defensive. "There are a few very sensitive areas in my life and my housekeeping is one of them." Then under her breath she muttered, "My weight is another."

87

The young woman took a bottle of furniture polish from Shirley's hand. "You're hardly lazy or a bad housekeeper. In fact, this is the easiest job I've got. You do all my work before I ever get here."

"No, I don't!" Shirley protested.

"Oh, yes you do. I sometimes wonder why you even have me come. But I figure every woman can use a boost now and then."

This woman was so familiar with Shirley's personal domain - her bathrooms, her bedroom, her kitchen - that Shirley felt a little intruded upon, but she only had herself to blame.

"You seem to understand," Shirley said slowly. "You don't think I'm lazy. You don't think I just hire help so I can relax and let you do the work. Do you?"

"Not at all. I have other clients whose houses are true disaster areas. Those women don't apologize for having me come and help them. That's the point of my job, isn't it?"

"I suppose so," answered Shirley. "It's just that our budget is so tight, I feel guilty for spending any money on help when I should be doing the work myself."

"So are you firing me?"

"Oh, no! What I am doing is trying to justify to you why I deserve your help. It really does give me that boost you talked about."

"Shirley, you don't owe me any explanations. You work hard and I think you deserve all the help that you can get."

Then the young woman continued to spout wisdom. "I know my mother and both of my grandmothers hired help with their house work, and neither of them even worked outside their homes."

That made Shirley think about something she hadn't thought about all of her adult life. Her own mother had hired a teenage neighbor girl when Shirley was a child. She helped with the laundry and most of the heavy work. And if her memory was working, Shirley was sure that her maternal grandmother had an actual live-in housekeeper to help with all of the chores.

"You know what?" Shirley said, her whole demeanor changing, "I think I'm going to take my little girl to the park for the rest of the afternoon and just let you do your job."

"Sounds like a great idea to me," said the housekeeper.

But before she left, Shirley made a telephone call - to her mother. "Mom, I might not be the mighty tradition breaker that I think I am."

*L*ate that night, even after the dryer had stopped, Shirley lay awake - feeling better about herself and her life than she could ever remember.

The afternoon in the park had turned into an evening picnic with the entire family. She came home to a clean house and no stress.

At this very moment, Shirley felt like the most blessed woman on the planet.

She nudged Stan with her elbow. "Honey, are you awake?"

"Huh?" he mumbled.

She kissed him softly on the lips. "Will you do me a favor?"

"What do you want?"

"I want you to validate me."

"What?"

"I want you to validate me. You know, make me feel appreciated. Acknowledged. Like a whole woman."

Now Stan was sitting up, rubbing the sleep from his eyes. "Shirley, you're up in the night. "

She kissed him again. "I know what time it is, but you're the last piece of my puzzle."

Stan didn't even pretend to understand. But he reached out and took her in his arms. This time he kissed her. "How's that for validation?"

"It's a start," Shirley said, kissing him back.

*T*hree weeks later Shirley was two weeks late. That scared her a little because her body worked to a 28 day cycle like a banker works 9 to 5.

"I think I might be pregnant," she announced to Stan, after she was sure he was sound asleep.

Wrong again.

Stan bolted up in bed like he had just had a wave of electricity run through him. "You think you might be *WHAT? When? How?*"

"Pregnant. A few weeks ago. I think you know *how.*"

There was an uncertain moment of dark silence before Shirley felt Stan's arms pull her close to him. "I know. It must have been that night you asked me to validate you."

"Probably," Shirley replied, "but that's not exactly what I meant."

"Well, it worked, didn't it?"

Shirley didn't respond. Men could be. . .

. . .but then so could women.

Stan held Shirley for a long, long time, assuring her how thrilled he was. Then he fell asleep - perfectly content. Shirley rolled him over on his side and scratched his back until he started to snore.

She turned on the lamp by her bedside. Then she reached into her nightstand and took out a well-worn manila envelope. She scattered the contents on the quilt across her lap.

She reached for the puzzle piece with Stan's name on it, but could not bring herself to glue it on the matte board - not permanently anyway.

Maybe that's because validation in a marriage was a two-way, never-ending process, she thought.

There was a new envelope lying there among her treasures. It had arrived this afternoon from the 1-900 VAL-DATE people. She opened it and read a once-in-a-lifetime offer to purchase a study course and video on "how to seek and find validation." If you had any further questions you could call the 1-900 number for *only* $3.95 per minute.

Shirley crumpled the advertisement and tossed it into a nearby garbage can.

Then she looked at her puzzle. It had not turned out at all like she had planned. There were pieces missing. Some changed. Others fit perfectly. More like a work in progress than a product finished.

Shirley decided that tomorrow she would have it framed and then hang it in some prominent place - the bathroom maybe.

Every time she looked at it, she would see how significant each piece was? What about the new pieces that would become necessary as new people entered her life?

How mistaken she had been to imagine every piece fitting perfectly into place. That wasn't her life. That wasn't reality.

Reality was ever changing, ever learning, and ever growing. Her life was a puzzle, and how boring it would be if all of the pieces were cut the same and fit neatly together.

As for validation, well she wasn't quite sure she even understood the meaning of the word anymore. Close, but not quite there. . .

Validate Me Quick!

No, the validation puzzle hadn't turned out at all like she had planned. But then she was learning to be grateful for life's little surprises.

She tucked everything carefully back into her envelope, placed it in her drawer, turned out the light and snuggled up against Stan. Maybe tomorrow she would glue his puzzle piece down permanently.

On second thought, maybe she would just velcro it in!

About The Author

Toni Sorenson Brown is a wife and mother of two daughters and three sons (ten and under). She is one of the most awarded family and children's portrait artists in that genre. She also oversees the operation of a publishing company and tries to author two of her own books each year. She teaches and lectures across the nation on publishing and photography. Her work appears regularly in national women's magazines.

She is fiercely devoted to her family and friends, even when they too often ask, "How come you always look so tired?"